From My Point Of View

Ten Dialogues On The Passion

Rolland R. Reece

CSS Publishing Company, Inc., Lima, Ohio

Library of Congress Cataloging-in-Publication Data

Reece, Rolland R., 1927-
   From my point of view : ten dialogues on the passion / Rolland R. Reece.
    p. cm.
   ISBN 0-7880-1935-X (pbk. : alk. paper)
   1. Jesus Christ—Passion. 2. Jesus Christ—Biography—Passion week. 3. Bible.
N.T. Gospels—Biography. I.Title.
   BT431.3 .R44 2003
   232.96—dc21

                                         2002151407

For more information about CSS Publishing Company resources, visit our website at www.csspub.com or e-mail us at custserv@csspub.com or call (800) 241-4056.

ISBN 0-7880-1935-X   PRINTED IN U.S.A.

*This book is dedicated to Lillian Jolly
for her countless hours typing, editing,
copying, collating, assembling, and all
the other things that dedicated secretaries do.
Her helpfulness cannot be measured.*

Table Of Contents

Introduction   7

Dialogue 1   Peter   9

Dialogue 2   Judas   15

Dialogue 3   Barabbas and Simon of Cyrene   21

Dialogue 4   Mary Magdalene   27

Dialogue 5   Thomas   33

Dialogue 6   Caiaphas   39

Dialogue 7   Pilate   45

Dialogue 8   Nicodemus and Joseph of Arimethea   53

Dialogue 9   Mary, Mother of Jesus   61

Dialogue 10   John, the Beloved Disciple   69

Scriptural References   77

Introduction

From My Point Of View presents twelve persons who played crucial roles in the death/resurrection event of Jesus Christ. These biographical sketches are intended to add flesh and blood to people whose names have long been familiar to us. Most of the presentations use two voices, one as a narrator giving background information, and a second as the personality talking for himself or herself. While the tone is dramatic, great care has been taken to stay within the scope of the scripture.

Use of the presentation is appropriate for mid-week or Sunday evening services during the Lenten season. These sketches could be the basis for a special Lenten Bible study series. A pastor might choose to use them for a sermon series. One youth group rearranged the material of one of the personalities to create parts for five or six voices.

Traditional sermons and illustrations have a tendency to press these personalities into one-dimensional, cardboard figures. Students and worshipers will appreciate the opportunity to know more about the humanity of these familiar names, thereby relating them more easily to their own lives.

RRR

Peter

Narrator: We do not know where Peter was on the day his Master hung from the cross. He may have been brooding in some darkened room, too humiliated by his cowardice, too deeply stung by his horrendous failure to seek the light of day. However, it is more likely that Peter was a part of that disparate gathering that watched until Jesus breathed no more. Peter, by nature, was not a loner. He needed to be with people, especially those closest to him.

He was not a man given to introspection and contemplation, but one who acted. He would much rather move into a situation with both fists flying than sit back and scheme a reasoned approach. It would be nearly impossible for Peter to remain away from the scene of the Master's death. The love of the Master whom he deeply cherished and the faint, lingering hope that he might still do something to free him would compel him to draw near.

Of all the persons who played a part in the death of Jesus, there is no one with whom we can so easily identify as Peter. Not only do we know more about him than the others, but he is such a wonderfully complex and variable person that there is at least one facet of his personality that causes each of us to exclaim, "That's just like me." While it would be an error to skip lightly over the historic achievements of his life, it may well be that the real lasting effectiveness of this man is bound up in the fact that we can see ourselves in him. This is a deeply painful experience at times, but the eventual outcome is characterized by hope.

Peter: I'm Peter.

I'm not sure that I should be here this evening; we're not exactly alike. I'm rough and tumble; you appear to be rather sedate. I work as a fisherman — I know the Sea of Galilee like the back of my hand. I don't know if any of you have ever seen the Sea of

Galilee. When I preach in the Court of the Gentiles, on the south side of the Temple, I need to keep an eye out for the Pharisees. They have already thrown me into jail several times. I don't believe you are being watched by your government or your denomination tonight.

I live right up against life. I'm shielded from nothing. No one is concerned with my rights when I'm imprisoned and chained. There is precious little medical help to aid me in fighting off the ravages of disease. I travel by foot, occasionally by boat. I work with my hands. I sit upon stone. I sleep on a mat. Meals are prepared when we become hungry, or when we get food. A lot of my time is spent meeting the needs of the moment. It's only been since I met Jesus that I even think of a future beyond the next catch of fish. In Capernaum we don't retire. We work until we can work no longer.

As I prepared for this evening it occurred to me that it may be in matters of the heart and passion where we are most alike.

It's certainly true that I am remembered most for my horrendous failures and *faux pas*. When I blundered, the whole world knew it, or so it seemed to me. Yes, I'm the one who denied knowing Christ to save my own skin. I failed to stand up to a serving girl, or answer some men, unknown to me, as I tried to stay warm by a nighttime fire. Do you remember reading about the time I jumped overboard to walk on water? Save for Christ, I would have drowned. I was scared to death!

Narrator: Through the imaginative skill of one writer, some background has been laid for interpreting this shocking experience. Andrew, Peter's brother, reveals that when Peter was a young boy he fell off a fishing vessel at sea. The severe scolding he received for being so careless, accompanied by the trauma of having nearly lost his life, brought to birth in him a giant fear, a fear he could never quite face — a fear he tried desperately to hide behind a mask of reckless courage.

So when the disciples were caught at sea in a violent storm, Peter saw Jesus miraculously walking on water. He cried out from his hidden fear to be allowed to walk on the water to the side of

Jesus. He wanted to be safe! Even though Jesus encouraged him, he was so terrorized by the past that he began sinking almost immediately. In his desperation he revealed something of that fear and cried out to Jesus to save him.

Peter: I'm also the one who gave Jesus an argument against his foot-washing ceremony. I made it an issue of my humility and pride — when it wasn't my issue at all. It was a powerful gift from the hand of the Master, who only wished to serve me.

I acted on impulse, never giving a second thought. Without a moment's hesitation, I proposed building three altars on the occasion when Jesus, Moses, and Elijah conferred on the Mount of Transfiguration. Well, what would you have done?

While our Master was teaching one day about the high cost of discipleship, I blurted out, "What's the pay-off for those of us who have given up everything?" There is nothing subtle about me.

On another day I took it upon myself to call Jesus down for talking about the approaching day of his death. Who wants to hear about that?

And when the temple guard came to apprehend Jesus, in an instant I grabbed a nearby sword and began flailing away. I managed only to cut off the ear of one of the soldiers. It was hardly a military victory.

When the news came that Jesus had risen from the tomb, another disciple and I had a foot race to see who would get there first. He won, but stayed outside in deference to the sacredness of the event and place. I ran on in. I wanted to see for myself! As I said, there is nothing subtle about me.

Because I acted on impulse, I often got myself in trouble. Invariably it was Jesus who bailed me out. How angry he often became with me — but once his anger was spent, he cared for me as before. He continued to rely on me — that's right — rely on me. In fact, the very first time we met he revealed that I would build his church. He knew something about me that even I didn't know.

Narrator: It was a beautiful and moving moment. It was the occasion when Peter correctly identified Jesus as "The Messiah, the

Son of the living God," and Jesus replied, "Blessed are you, Simon son of Jonah! For flesh and blood has not revealed this to you, but my Father in heaven. And I tell you, you are Peter, and on this rock I will build my church, and the gates of Hades will not prevail against it" (Matthew 16:16-18).

Can you conceive of the Lord Jesus determining to lay the future of the Church upon such a person as Peter? One who was ridden with fear, who chose to escape from life, and at the crucial hour deny the one he loved most. What a reckless and extravagant faith Jesus had! And the Master was not disappointed.

We know that on that day that Jesus was crucified he thought of the future, for he gave counsel to his people and made provision for the care of his loved ones. We would like to think that sometime during the course of that event his eyes met those of Peter and that he spoke of the tomorrows that lay ahead. That something happened between the two of them is a certainty, for when they next fell into conversation, following the resurrection, Jesus continued to build upon his original estimate of Peter.

Peter: After breakfast Jesus said to me: "Simon son of John, do you love me more than these?" And I said to him, "Yes, Lord; you know that I love you." Jesus said to me, "Feed my lambs." A second time Jesus said to me, "Simon son of John, do you love me?" Again I said to him, "Yes, Lord; you know that I love you." Jesus said to me, "Tend my sheep." He said to me a third time, "Do you love me?" Rather brusquely I said to him, "Lord, you know everything; you know that I love you." Finally he said to me, "Feed my sheep" (John 21:15-17).

And I, who couldn't speak up to a servant girl, found my tongue to speak boldly to the Council.

Later, on the Day of Pentecost, I witnessed to our faith, and 3000 people joined our community. John and I healed a beggar. I raised Tabitha from the dead. People lay on the street to catch my shadow as I passed by, hoping my image would cure them.

And there was the vision. It was a vision of unclean animals being lowered from above on a sheet. I was invited to eat of these beasts — but they were unclean according to our law. So I refused.

12

Then a voice spoke to me that I should not swear against that which the Lord has made. As events unraveled, it became clear I was actually being told that the Gentiles were proper persons to become Christians.

I spoke of this before the church in Jerusalem and won the day. Later I backed away from what I learned, and Paul had to rebuke me. Even in the best of times the old Peter would reappear.

Also, Jesus, on the occasion of the breakfast, said to me, "Very truly, I tell you, when you were younger, you used to fasten your belt and go wherever you wished. But when you grow old, you will stretch out your hands, and someone else will fasten a belt around you and take you where you do not wish to go." (He said this to me to indicate the kind of death by which I would glorify God.) After that he said, "Follow me" (John 21:18-19).

Narrator: It has been said, "A saint is not a man who never fails; a saint is a man who gets up and goes on again every time he fails."

During his last imprisonment an angel came and led Peter to freedom. It was time for him to leave Jerusalem. After greeting his friends, he left the city heading north and west. He spent the rest of his life preaching in Antioch, Corinth, and other cities in Asia Minor. Eventually he made his way to Rome and became a victim of the persecution conducted under Nero's rule. The year was 64 A.D. He requested and was granted permission to be crucified upside down. This he did out of respect for his Master.

Judas

Defender: As children we had little trouble understanding Judas. He was the most evil man that ever lived and that was that. As adults we still have a desire to see him so simply, for such a viewpoint neatly answers several questions we have. However, we have an uneasy feeling that there is something suspect about such a simple solution. Life, as we find it, is rarely black or white — often it is a mix of black and white.

Yet the lure to see Judas as the worst of men — or an oddity even among the most satanic of personalities — is strong. It helps explain how a man might sink to betray such a one as our Master. Even the Gospel writers couldn't resist adding words to persuade a reader to conjure up the kind of personality that could only have been the creation of Satan.

If we can establish — once and for all — that Judas is some kind of immoral freak, then we have gone a long way in establishing that his evil will not be found in others. Most certainly we don't want to find out that such a spirit may be within us.

For this occasion let us set aside our stereotypes and simplifications of Judas and start with a fresh, clean page. Judas, like all other disciples, was selected by Jesus only after a long period of thought and prayer. Apparently he was a man who exhibited a strong potential for leadership. His native village was Kerioth, which made him the only Judean in the inner circle. All the others came from Galilee. For over two years he was a faithful and effective member of that little band clustered about Jesus. We find no evidence that he created any distrust or disloyalty within the fellowship.

That the disciples were lacking in suspicion of Judas was clearly revealed on the night of the Last Supper. Jesus announced that one of the group was going to betray him. This did not cause all eyes to fall on Judas automatically, as if to say, "We knew it all along." Rather the members of the inner circle asked, "Surely not I, Lord?" (Matthew 26:22). Even when Jesus identified Judas as the betrayer to the beloved disciple, there was still a lack of recognition and belief that he could be the one. And many within that circle had no inkling that it was Judas even when he left early from the supper to set into motion his deadly plan. Later that night he would bring the temple guard to apprehend Jesus in the Garden of Gethsemane.

Judas wasn't Satan incarnate. He was a person, with all the potential for good and evil found in any other person. To make him a satanic stick figure reflects on Jesus' judgment and the efficacy of his prayers. It's totally unrealistic in terms of our experience and knowledge of people to say that he was completely without a will of his own, or that he was the unwitting instrument of the force of evil. But then how do we explain his betrayal?

Some have said it was the love of money that caused him to betray. Tradition says that he once was a man of means, but lost much of it in following Jesus. When he came to the point of financial desperation, the thirty pieces of silver looked good, so he decided to sell out. This idea lacks credibility when we discover that was the price of any slave on the market — and Jesus wasn't just any man. He was badly wanted. It has been estimated that Jesus should have brought at least five times the thirty pieces of silver.

Perhaps Judas was suffering from alienation. Being the only Judean among all the Galileans, he may have been rejected. Finally resenting his isolation deeply enough, perhaps he decided to retaliate by bringing the whole venture to an end. We do strange things out of revenge.

Again he may have sensed that Jesus was plunging into deep trouble and therefore decided to turn king's evidence to save his own skin. The chief priests may have assured him safety as well as money, if he would but reveal to them how they could lay hold of Jesus without causing a riot.

Still he may have betrayed Jesus from fear. Jesus could see Judas for what he was, even though the disciples remained blind to him. The Master made him very uncomfortable. He was driven to kill the one person who knew him for what he was.

Yet another idea is that he fancied himself a protector of the people. Fearing that Jesus would lead the Jewish populace into a foolish blood bath against the forces of Rome, he decided to end Jesus' mad dreaming of a heavenly kingdom here on earth by turning him in.

Or is it that Judas was the unwitting pawn of Old Testament prophecy? This was his destiny. He was the one to draw history's "short straw." Therefore, so be it. In this instance a question arises within us: Did our God of mercy turn his back to make "things work out right"?

The most likely explanation for Judas' motivation comes from the late Dr. Leslie Weatherhead of London Temple, England. Dr. Weatherhead contends that Judas was a rabid nationalist, which fits the tenor of his home village, Kerioth. When he first heard Jesus speak of the coming new age, the new kingdom, Judas immediately began to believe Jesus was precisely the man for whom he yearned. The days, weeks, and months that followed were like a dream come true. Deeply he felt the emotional strength of his Master's teaching. Joyfully he observed the bonds of loyalty meld together the inner circle. Excitedly he noted the power of Jesus and the wonder of his miracles. Expectantly he counted the growing number who came to hear and see the carpenter's son. The passion within his breast began to mount as he looked forward to the day when Jesus would set his people against the Romans, drive them literally into the sea, and establish the Jewish nation free and unfettered from any foreign domination. How could Rome withstand the strength of this man of miracles? The days of King David would soon return.

Then doubts began to enter Judas' heart. Little ones at first, then later larger, more persistent ones. He was disturbed by Jesus' soft approach when the times called for bold, striking action. It irritated him that the Master would take time to deal with ones and twos, when there were thousands to be marshaled into marching troops. He had the power — no doubt of this — but he seemed so dilatory. Imagine taking an hour at noonday to talk to an oft-married woman about her unhappy life. He should have sent her on her way — he had more important things to accomplish.

17

Then came the idea — the grand scheme — that, put into action, would stir the Master into taking his nation's leadership. He would force Jesus into action by putting the chief priests onto him. Jesus would have to retaliate and this would start the process that would lead to the establishment of his kingdom, for no one would dare withstand the priests without attempting to grasp all the power available.

So it was that Judas, blinded by a dream rooted in fantasy, sold the Master for thirty pieces of silver.

How we despise the man who came to the garden so casually and so cheerfully met his Master with a greeting and a kiss. But if we understand his motivation, we can sense that for him this was the moment that the great Jewish nation would be born. He could already taste the glory of the new morning.

Then the unbelievable took place. Jesus didn't resist his captors. He accepted their chains without so much as a dissenting word. He ordered his followers to lay down their arms, and he accepted his fate. Judas could not believe what he witnessed. It just couldn't be true. Slowly it crashed in upon his mind that he didn't really understand Jesus. What he wanted from Jesus was a leader to accomplish his own personal dreams and ambitions. He didn't want Jesus for who he was. He had sided with Jesus to use him. And in his effort to use him, he would take his life.

When the weight of truth fell upon Judas, he decided he couldn't live with himself. In one account we read that he hanged himself on one of that dry land's knobby trees. In another that he threw himself down from some stony precipice upon sharp rocks below that tore out his bowels.

The greatest tragedy of his life is not his betrayal, but his failure to turn to the Master for forgiveness and healing. With his eyes Judas had seen the Master forgive others, but he never grasped that it was possible for him as well.

He stood in the presence of beauty and chose not to see.

He stood in the presence of truth and chose to believe a lie.

He stood in the presence of hope and chose destruction.

Mary Todd Lincoln dressed down the President's guard: "Where were you? You had no business being careless." Then she paused, "It's not you I can't forgive; it's the assassin."

Then Tad, the President's son, spoke up, "If Pa had lived, he would have forgiven the man who shot him. Pa forgave everybody."

So did our Lord.

Judas failed to believe his Master's word. That is the legacy we need to destroy — not the man himself.

Barabbas and
Simon of Cyrene

Presenter: Two men were thrust into the trial and death of Jesus. They had no warning. They had no preparation. They responded from who they were.

Barabbas

Barabbas was the unlettered hero of many Israelites, a prisoner serving time for insurrection and murder. With courage marked more by daring than wisdom, he had led fiery bands of zealots into various battles and skirmishes against Roman forces. Their efforts were doomed to failure before they ever took place, but Barabbas nonetheless became a hero of the people, for he was a swashbuckling character who won immediate loyalty of men, the admiration of women, and the anger of Roman soldiers. He would undertake any risk, regardless how foolish, if it would somehow move the Jewish people one step closer to becoming an independent nation.

To people long oppressed, who had been forced to lick the boots of many conquerors, Barabbas seemed like a bright star, a promise in a world devoid of hope. When they received reports that he and his faithful men had plundered the quarters of the Roman soldiers or had ambushed a small company of Romans on patrol duty, their burdened lives would temporarily be given relief and joy. Barabbas was something of a Jewish Robin Hood. However, his animal cleverness was not enough, for on one occasion the Romans were successful in capturing and imprisoning him.

By chance (or was it by manipulation of the high priest?) Barabbas was brought out during the trial of Jesus to form the choice the people were given to release one man to freedom. This was a custom that was practiced under Pilate. Perhaps Pilate selected Barabbas believing that no one would call for his release, since Pilate himself would have never released him. But he forgot that he was Roman and his subjects were Jewish, and in their eyes Barabbas was a hero, not a scoundrel. Pilate was certain that the choice was stacked, and it was, but not in his favor. "Whom do you want me to release for you, Jesus Barabbas or Jesus who is called the Messiah?" (Matthew 27:17).

Barabbas stood grinning arrogantly, for he had nothing to lose. It was only by the wheel of fortune that he had come to this moment anyway. The sun sparkled upon his curly black hair and revealed a body that was as strong as spring steel in spite of imprisonment. He could have been saying, "Hey, who do you want me to go after?"

On the other hand, Jesus stood in silence. Though he was erect and tall, the anguish of the garden, the all-night trial under the high priest Caiaphas, the cursing and beating of the soldiers, and the total lack of sleep were beginning to take their toll. He felt no need to play to the crowd through an impish grin; his only concern was that of remaining faithful to his Father. That wasn't easily communicated through appearance.

Some people thought well enough of Jesus. After all, he had healed, performed miracles, and taught a highly ethical religion. But when compared with the strutting Barabbas — one who struck back at the enemy, who would not give in to the enemy under any circumstances — then Jesus seemed weak and ineffective. The day called for aggressive, forceful strength — not a philosophy of loving one's enemy. So the crowd shouted for the release of Barabbas.

Now we say, how foolish not to release Jesus. How criminal to kill a man who could grant life abundant. But on that day Barabbas was resplendent in his cockiness; he was the promise of a quick victory and restored national pride.

We never hear of Barabbas again.

Simon of Cyrene

To say that Simon was surprised would be the understatement of all history. He had journeyed a long distance to be in Jerusalem for the Feast of the Passover. His home city was Cyrene, which was located on the southern shore of the Mediterranean Sea —

due south of Corinth, Greece, and due west of Alexandria, Egypt. One source claims it was a 700-mile trip. My atlas measured it — somewhat as the crow flies — to be closer to 900 miles. Either one would be considered a long distance if we were to travel by car. But to go by small boat, or by animal, or by foot, would be a very long distance. It was not a journey to be taken lightly. Simon may have made it every five or ten years, or perhaps only once or twice in his lifetime.

It is present-day speculation that Simon may have been a black person. While there was a sizeable group of white Jews in Cyrene, there were native converts, who quite properly assumed Jewish names. In the book of Acts (13:1) it refers to a Symeon (or Simon) who was called Niger, a dark-skinned one, a black one — in connection with another believer from Cyrene. Since this is the only notation available, it may be too thin to establish that Simon was black. But one scholar points out that "there may be more evidence for this conclusion than any other."

Whatever his color, this man of deep faith had traveled a long distance to worship God at the feast of feasts. It was his ambition to enter the great temple, to join his voice with thousands of others in the saying of the *Shema*, to hear the scriptures read, and to celebrate once again Israel's deliverance from their oppressors. He had prepared himself through prayer and recounting the events of his people under the guidance of Moses. He had taken great precaution not to disqualify himself from the feast by becoming unclean through association with sinners, the diseased, or the maimed.

As Simon approached the beloved city, he was met by a tumult of voices risen to an hysterical pitch. He was soon engulfed by a surging mob that was shouting for the death of someone named "Jesus" whom they called "the king" in derision. Quickly he asked questions to get enough facts to be able to understand the situation.

At last his eye caught sight of the poor wretch straining under his burden as he climbed his way to the hill of death. No Jewish person touched him or his cross, for this would make them unclean for the festival, so they leaned on the Roman soldiers who surrounded Jesus to get close enough to spit on him or yell insults into his ear.

Simon watched transfixed. This was a horrible drama of people venting their hatred on someone who was a symbol of blasphemy. He found himself pulling back as if the man were a leper.

Then Jesus fell. The soldiers attempted to get him back on his feet, but to no avail. The beating and the scourging he had endured made Jesus too weak to continue. The centurion in charge had to think quickly for a solution to the dilemna. Roman soldiers, by law, were not permitted to carry a cross. He could not select a Jew, for they would be made unclean for the feast — besides, he couldn't risk the possibility of a riot if he chose one of them. As his mind raced for a solution, his eyes fell upon this foreign-looking man, dressed in the garb of another land. Without a second thought, he pulled his sword and tapped the man on the shoulder — blade flat — the symbol of conscription. The soldiers then laid hold of Simon, and instinctively he attempted to wrestle free of them, but he was no match for their strength. He pleaded with the one in charge not to do this. He explained all that he had done to get to Jerusalem. If he were compelled to carry this man's cross, he would be disqualified from the feast. "I may not return for ten years." The soldier ignored him. He knew no one would rise to his defense. He was a stranger. Who ever rushed to defend a stranger?

So Simon carried an *unexpected cross*. Even as the cutting weight of the cross piece dug into his shoulders, he couldn't believe this was happening. "It just can't be. I've come too far. I have given up too much — to think that the celebration should be taken from me in the snap of a finger. This must be a bad dream from which I'll waken."

Simon also carried an *unwanted cross*. How he loathed his task. The cross on his back denied him the goal for which he had so greatly yearned. Its very weight reminded him that all his time and effort had been spent in vain.

I remember how embarrassed the woman was. Her brother had squandered his life. Now he was ill and no one would take him in — not even his own children. So she took him in, and since her husband wouldn't let him in their house, she cleaned a place in a vacated chicken coop and nursed him to his death. As she explained to me, "Someone had to do this. Someone." How we dislike the unwanted crosses.

But Simon also carried the *cross of honor and glory*. And this is the miracle — that an unexpected and unwanted cross could become a cross of honor and glory. What happened that would make this dramatic change possible?

Since we have a record that Jesus spoke to others on that day — the weeping women, the thieves, the crowd, the beloved disciple — perhaps he also spoke to Simon. He may have indicated how deeply indebted he was to this stranger and thereby revealed that he understood something of the high price Simon was being forced to pay by this cruel act.

Perhaps the cross took on a different value, as Simon quietly observed this man for whom he was performing this favor. Never had he witnessed a man seeking forgiveness for those who abused him. How sensitively he talked with the thieves. How loving to respond to the care of his mother. Even so, it may have been the centurion's testimony that turned his thinking, "Truly this man was God's son" (Mark 15:39).

Something was communicated from Jesus to Simon. Somehow the unexpected and unwanted cross became the emblem of honor and glory. Simon became a Christian because of, not in spite of, the cross he was made to carry. How are we assured that this is true? He is listed among the prophets and teachers in the Antioch Church; furthermore his sons Rufus and Alexander both became leaders in the church. Both were thought to have traveled with Peter. Paul, in his letter to Rome, expresses appreciation not only for Rufus, but his mother as well (Mark 15:21; Romans 16:13).

Often when we think of accepting Christ, we think of what he can do for us. But there is another side in coming to Christ, and that is the offering of who we are to him. This may cause a violent struggle, for we often want to retain who we are for our own benefit.

Simon scored a great victory over himself on that unforgettable day, for he accepted the courage God offered him to give himself without reserve. That same victory can be ours.

25

Thou must have looked on Simon;
Turn, Lord, and look on me
'Til I shall see and follow
And bear thy cross for Thee.
— Harriet Ware Hall

Two men were thrust into the trial and death of Jesus. They had no warning. They had no preparation. They responded from who they were.

One vanished.

One believed.

Mary Magdalene

Narrator: The biblical record of Mary Magdalene is sparse. The few facts that are available are thin and, with the exception of the encounter of Mary and Jesus at the tomb, are lacking in substance.

However, Mary's name is recorded 144 times; nine of these are in listings of names. In eight of the lists, Mary's name is mentioned first, even ahead of the mother of the two disciples James and John, and Joanna the wife of Herod's steward, and many others. Even a cursory glance at these listings quickly discloses her importance to that early Christian community. First name was first placed.

We surmise from the biblical account that she possessed a deep and abiding affection for Jesus. She (and the other women as well) endured the unplanned, demanding travels of this group. From her home in Magdala they typically might travel through Galilee and Samaria into the northern part of Judea and finally into Jerusalem.

Whatever delays, hardships, or persecutions befell those early disciples, she also accepted without defection. She stood by silently, helplessly through the Last Supper, the torment of the garden, and the rigged and torturous trials. She stood at the cross. She gathered spices to prepare Jesus' body for burial and volunteered to stand watch at his grave. Her affection was no light or transitory love.

Mary Magdalene: I'm Mary of Magdala.

Magdala is my home city. It is located on the northwest shore of the Sea of Galilee and is the largest of the cities along the shoreline, although you may not find it listed on the New Testament map in the back of your Bible. Other cities such as Capernaum, Tiberius, Bethsaida, and Gennesaret are more closely associated with Jesus' ministry.

27

However, all that makes little difference to me, for what I remember is the day that Jesus freed me from seven demons that had overrun my mind and spirit. I understand that you speculate that I had epilepsy — grand mal seizures that came frequently. Of course I don't know about epilepsy. I only remember being unable to control my mind, unable to think things out, controlled by an endless stream of crazy images that I could not stop. Later my family told me how I babbled and foamed at the mouth, tore at my clothes, and was either unable or unwilling to wash myself. They were driven to treat me like a deranged animal. But what I clearly recall is that day when I emerged from my madness — blessed with clear thought and focused vision — to behold this smiling young man standing before me urging me to enter into the joy of life. How can I describe that to you? One moment I was struggling against all the gifts of life with no comprehension of their worth, and in the next moment, I was holding every gift of life against my breast realizing they were mine and that I was now empowered to engage in all the facets of human endeavor.

I went from point zero to 100. I flew from the darkest canyon to the highest mountaintop. All my family and friends I had lost for a while were mine again. Every precious item and nuance of life had been restored for my happiness. Can you imagine what that young man Jesus meant to me? Even now I can scarcely catch my breath. Gladly I followed him and his disciples. I listened to him teach, and when he asked me to become a part of his company, I never hesitated. My father was wealthy, which enabled me to provide — along with Joanna, Susanna, and many others — the resources we needed for Jesus' ministry.

These were the happiest days I had ever known. Of course traveling through Galilee, Samaria, and Judea into Jerusalem wasn't easy. Finding lodging, preparing food, keeping clothes clean, and tending to illness when you are on the road can be frustrating and sometimes overwhelming. However, when the Master taught on the hillside, healed the blind and the lame, set the Pharisees on their ear, or lifted a little child from death — what greater moments are there? Every sunrise opened my eyes to behold the next great day of my life. There is no one like Jesus. No one.

Narrator: One of the great disservices accomplished by the Church, in later centuries, was linking Mary Magdalene with one or more of the prostitutes whose stories also appear in the Gospels. Her name does not appear in any of those accounts. It is conjectured that because her name, along with other women, is listed in the first verses of the eighth chapter of Luke, following the powerful story of Jesus forgiving the sinful woman who bathed his feet with her tears and dried them with her hair, that apparently this woman was Mary. But there is no evidence to substantiate this. (So it is true of the accounts of other fallen women.) None can be linked to this delightful, devoted woman from Magdala. Perhaps it was thought that her passion for Jesus could emerge only from a woman who had been so dramatically rescued from a life of moral bankruptcy.

Indeed the Western Church, convinced of her sexual depravity and her eternal rescue, established the Magdalene Homes for Fallen Women. This further cemented the idea of her sexual immorality in our minds. A *Webster's Dictionary*, under the word "Magdalene," says, "a reformed and repentant prostitute." The Eastern or Orthodox Church never categorized her that way. We have no need to sneer at prostitutes, but we do need to let Mary Magdalene be who she is in the biblical account.

Mary Magdalene: As we drew near to Jerusalem, we became alarmed. Any time we came to the Holy City our emotions ran high, but this time fear caused us to be tentative and cautious. It was not business as usual. Our entrance upon its worn cobbled streets was fraught with meaning. Our concern was to be found not only in what Jesus had said, but in his determination to come here. It wasn't that he didn't hear the warning in our voices, it was as if he listened to a more insistent voice that we couldn't hear.

Though we women were not far away, we couldn't hear what was said in the Upper Room when Jesus celebrated the Feast and revealed to his disciples the new covenant in his blood. If only we could have heard those words the first time they were spoken. Judas left early, but we didn't attach too much meaning to that, for he was consistently something of a loner. When they left and headed for one of their favorite haunts, the Garden of Gethsemane, we followed at a distance. We saw their lights flickering now and then, but a silence settled over the hillside and we huddled together to ward off some of the chill of the night. Perhaps we fell asleep; I'm not sure.

Suddenly there was a growing sound of people — were they soldiers? — mounting the hill from another direction. Their torches lit up the place where the disciples and Jesus had gathered. We could hear shouting and the voice of Jesus. We ran to the spot where they were, only to see Jesus being taken away. What is happening? — we wanted to know. But the soldiers were moving Jesus quickly toward the city and the disciples were not to be seen.

We learned later that Peter did follow after the military entourage as it escorted Jesus to the home of the high priest. The hillside was empty. No one was there. We had been abandoned and we were terrified.

Cautiously we re-entered the city and went to the homes in which we were staying. Eventually we made contact with some of the disciples and learned what had taken place. Then from the clattering of people assembling we picked up the trail Jesus was compelled to follow from the High Priest Caiaphas' home to Herod's palace to the Via Dolorosa. The disciples had every reason to hide, for their lives were in danger. We women — especially Jesus' mother and her sister — were not viewed as dangerous or enemies of the faith. We were just women, after all; it was all right for us to follow along weeping, wailing, mourning.

I remember standing behind Mother Mary at the cross thinking this was the longest day of my life. At first I was overwhelmed with anger. I wanted to strike something or someone. Then sorrow and tears came and eventually I shuddered into a state of numbness. I must have stood as a lifeless statue for hours.

When at last John led Jesus' mother away and the soldier pierced Jesus' side with a sword, then I came out of my lethargy. I went to the cross and rested my head on the Master's feet and prayed that somehow all this man-savior had been would not come to naught. Afterward I was disturbed by Joseph of Arimathea and Nicodemus, who had gained permission to remove Jesus from the cross and bury him. They had to move quickly for there were just three hours left until sundown and the beginning of the Sabbath.

After the men freed Jesus from the cross, I held his head in my lap and then assisted Joseph and Nicodemus in preparing the Master's body for burial. I watched where they went and took note of the place where he was buried. Because we had to work fast, I knew we would need to return and add more spices and preservatives to the wrapping. I stumbled back into the city on leaden legs. My spirit was numb.

Narrator: Matthew, Mark, and Luke tell of the women — Mary Magdalene, Mary, mother of James, another Mary, Salome, Joanna, and yet other women — going to the grave. Each Gospel lists Mary Magdalene first, but after her name the lists are quite different. At the tomb they met an angel or a young man who told them:

> *Do not be alarmed, you are looking for Jesus of Nazareth, who was crucified. He has been raised; he is not here. Look there is the place they laid him. But go, tell his disciples and Peter that he is going ahead of you to Galilee; there you will see him, just as he told you.* — Mark 16:6, 7

In Matthew, Mary Magdalene and the other Mary see Jesus following this speech, and take hold of his feet to worship him. Then he needs to re-instruct them to go tell the disciples. In Mark the women become afraid and tell no one, and in Luke they carry out their duty, but the brethren think it is an idle tale.

It's the Gospel of John that completes the story of Mary Magdalene.

Mary Magdalene: I returned to the Master's tomb on the morning of the first day of the week to complete his burial preparation. But I found the tomb empty and was alarmed and returned to the city to tell Peter and John. They ran to the grave and I followed as best I could. When they witnessed its emptiness for themselves and began to speculate about its possible meaning, they decided to return to the others.

I stayed at the tomb and began weeping.

31

Narrator as Jesus: "Woman, why are you weeping?"

Mary Magdalene: "They have taken away my Lord, and I do not know where they have laid him." Then I turned around and saw a man that I assumed to be the caretaker, and I said: "Sir, if you have carried him away, tell me where you have laid him, and I will take him away."

Narrator as Jesus: "Mary."

Mary Magdalene: "Teacher." (*Reaches out to him*)

Narrator as Jesus: "Do not hold on to me, because I have not yet ascended to the Father. But go to my brothers and say to them, I am ascending to my Father, to my God and your God" (John 20:11-17).

Mary Magdalene: How great that unbelievable moment, the miracle of all miracles! How I yearned to embrace him. But it had to remain a joy that wouldn't reach its fullest expression. Nevertheless, I went to the disciples with the best news ever: "I have seen the Lord!" (John 11:18b). From that day on our community was never the same.

Narrator: Mary Magdalene rose to a high place of distinction in that early Christian fellowship. She was the pivotal figure in Christ's resurrection. She was the first to see him alive, the first to speak to him, and the first to deliver the good news: "I have seen the Lord."

In the days following Jesus' death and resurrection she was no doubt with those women who prayed with the disciples seeking the will of God for the future. It's not difficult to imagine that she became an excellent witness.

The Greek Orthodox tradition tells us that she accompanied John, the beloved disciple, to Ephesus, where she apparently lived a devoted Christian life and died. Later, according to the same account, she was buried in Constantinople.

Her message is a simple one: Live the joy of the faith, today, right where you are!

Thomas

Presenter: If it had been left up to Matthew, Mark, and Luke we wouldn't be talking about Thomas today. When they revealed the list of disciples, after Jesus prayed for and selected them, they placed Thomas in the seventh or eighth position of the inner twelve. That is all Matthew and Mark had to say of him — they listed him and nothing more. Luke, in the book of Acts, places Thomas at Christ's Ascension; then, when reporting of the disciples' return to the Upper Room, to devote themselves to prayer, he moves his name up two places in the list of twelve. Then he tells us nothing more.

It's the Gospel of John that makes Thomas memorable. In his telling Thomas becomes a fascinating and challenging figure. We have hung the adjective *doubting* on his name — to come up with *doubting Thomas*. But that's only part of the man, and perhaps when all is known, the smaller part.

Resigned, but brave. First we find Thomas in the Gospel of John as a courageous stoic. He is one who has a horrible fate to meet, but will throw back his shoulders, hold his head up high, and move forward regardless of the cost.

Jesus receives word that his friend Lazarus is ill and therefore he plans to visit him. But Lazarus lives close to Jerusalem and, knowing that there are people lying in wait for the Master, Thomas and the other disciples attempt to persuade him not to go. Jesus decides to proceed anyway; there is no holding him back.

This prompts Thomas to say in a resigned yet brave voice, "Let us also go, that we may die with him" (John 11:16). He has no hope that this journey will work out well, but he has cast his lot with Jesus and will stay by him.

Let's get the details straight. A second time the Gospel of John focuses on Thomas is just after Jesus has announced that he

33

will leave the disciples. He concludes his remarks by revealing that he is going to prepare a place for them so they may follow. "In my Father's house are many rooms" (John 14:2).

While some of the hearers might have been excited by this prospect, Thomas was skeptical: "Lord, we do not know where you are going. How can we know the way?" (John 14:5). Our Master may have a good idea, but let's be practical — we will get lost if he doesn't name the place and the road that leads to it. (Does this sound like us?) What are we talking about here, North Royaltown or Doylestown? Are we taking Interstate 76 or Route 18? Who's going to buy the gas?

I'll believe it when I see it. The third time we meet Thomas in the Gospel of John is following the death Jesus. Thomas had left the Christian company. As a consequence, when Jesus visited his disciples, Thomas was absent. When his friends explained what had happened, he told them, "Unless I see the mark of the nails in his hands, and put my hand in his side, I will not believe" (John 20:25). His no-nonsense kind of approach would not accept their testimony. Thomas didn't see life poetically; he saw it in facts and figures.

While there was only one Thomas in biblical history, there have been many persons who have ended up with the same question. Just what is this resurrection business all about? How can we possibly believe in it? To this end Thomas sounds like modern man. Let's take note of three facts about this most famous of all doubters.

1. It wasn't his doubting that caused him a problem; it was his absence. After Jesus' crucifixion, Thomas decided to break company with the disciples. Some people prefer to grieve alone, but before healing finally comes, the grief will need to be shared, for grief is born of separation and its healing is in union. Thomas was a loner. He would shed his tears in the darkness of his closet.

Thomas cut himself off from that early band of Christians, so when Jesus appeared, he wasn't present. He had positioned himself out of the reach of healing.

2. Whatever else Thomas might have been, he was honest. When at last he returned to the disciples and heard what they had

34

to say, he doubted their message. "Unless I see ... the print of the nails ... I will not believe." There is no uncertainty here. If I don't see it, I don't believe it.

This is so much better than to have doubts and yet follow all the forms of a vital faith without ever raising any of the questions. That is to say, I have my doubts, but rather than look into them, I'll pretend they are not there and be on my way.

Our faith has never been judgmental about doubt. Indeed it often appears on the threshold of still a greater faith. Alfred Lloyd Tennyson once said, "There lives more faith in honest doubt, believe me, than in half the creeds."

Psalm 73 is a movement from doubt to faith. This experience is found in the story of Jeremiah. Certainly Paul revealed it. He wrote that he was crushed, nonetheless nothing would ever separate him from the love of God.

There is faith in honest doubt. This we find in the book of Job. Even when Job shouted at the Lord, his God was more preferred by Job than any of his so-called "comforters," who represented traditional answers and forms. They were singing, "The old-time religion is good enough for me," and he was saying that it didn't meet the needs of his situation. They had theology, but he had something of God. They had all the answers, and Job had all the questions, and there was a more helpful religion in his questions than in all their answers.

3. When Thomas was confronted with the truth, he responded to it without reservation. Thomas rejoined the little band of Christians and when Christ appeared again, he was there. Christ, knowing of Thomas' doubts, invited him to satisfy himself by touching his nail prints and the hole in his side: "Do not doubt, but believe." Thomas didn't need to touch Jesus, but cried from his heart, "My Lord and my God!" To which Jesus replied, "Have you believed because you have seen me? Blessed are those who have not seen and yet have come to believe" (John 20:27-29). Please note, Thomas was able to rise above himself!

Truth has a non-changing quality about it, but not our approach to truth. Some years ago the Bible and the Christian faith were not to be questioned or doubted — they were the truth and that was that. Our generation sounds more like Thomas: "Unless I see the print of the nails ... I will not believe!" We assume that truth must be demonstrated or proven and if it can't be, then it is suspect as truth.

Still others feel that unless there is a strong emotional pull, the truth is on shaky ground.

Yet others rely on experience as the reliable guide to truth. Without this kind of support it is best to view whatever the matter is dimly.

This brings us to the issue before Thomas — the resurrection of Christ. Did it happen, or didn't it? If only we had the opportunity of Thomas — to stand before Jesus with an invitation to touch. Dare we believe Thomas?

Martin Niemoller, in Dachau, preached to eight fellow prisoners. He told them that proof of the resurrection is not possible. "It can only be certified through testimony, and thus we admit by faith, or deny it by unbelief."

Dr. Murdo Ewen McDonald, a Presbyterian preacher, was chaplain for American prisoners during World War II and was greatly loved by the soldiers. He told of how he learned about the invasion of D Day. Early in the morning he was awakened by an American shouting in his ear, "The Scotsman wants to see you — it's terribly important."

McDonald ran over to a barbed wire fence that separated the British and American camps, where MacNeil, who was in touch with the BBC by underground radio, was waiting for him. He spoke two words in Gaelic, meaning, "They have come."

McDonald ran back to the American camp and started waking up the soldiers. He said again and again, "They have come!" The reaction was incredible. Men jumped up and started to shout. They hugged each other. They ran outdoors. They rolled on the ground in joy. The German guards thought they were crazy. They were still prisoners. Nothing outwardly had changed. Inwardly, however, they knew everything was different. They believed the messenger.

Do we believe Thomas? Can we say, "My Lord and my God"?

We are glad it was Thomas who had to answer the question, "Is this the resurrected Jesus, or not?" We don't feel he would be

36

manipulated into a "yes" answer unless he was convinced that it was Jesus standing in front of him. Another disciple might have been hoodwinked or sweet-talked, but not Thomas.

There is one more meeting of Thomas and Jesus, according to the Gospel of John. It was the same occasion when Jesus prepared breakfast on the beach and had a heart-to-heart talk with Peter. There were just seven disciples in attendance, but it's interesting to note that Thomas is listed second, right after Peter. At least in the eyes of John, Thomas had gained stature.

On the fateful day when Thomas exclaimed, "My Lord and my God," Jesus said, "Have you believed because you have seen me? Blessed are those who have not seen and yet have come to believe."

Which brings the matter down to us. We who haven't seen the nail prints in his body, do we believe? Did Jesus rise triumphant over death?

At stake is our faith that we can rise above the many deaths and defeats that plague us throughout the living of our days. Are we doomed to hanging onto decreasing shreds of life, or dare we lift our arms in victory for whatever portion of life we still possess, for it still connects us to God who is our everlasting source of joy?

At stake, also, is our belief in eternal life. Jesus rose triumphant over death making it possible for us to rise triumphant over our death. How do we claim that promise? By believing that the Lord Jesus is our Savior and by giving our hearts to him. It comes down to belief.

We Christians have been hung out to dry by some members of the scientific/intellectual community because of our insistence on belief. Prove it to me, it is said, demonstrate it, make it logical/arguable — then I'll believe it. We are not duped. The excruciating and exquisite moments of decision are characterized by belief and faith, not proof.

Do we believe in the resurrection of Jesus Christ?

What is our answer?

Caiaphas

Narrator: If one person was more responsible for Jesus' death than any other, it would have to be Caiaphas. Caiaphas, the High Priest, was a man of far-reaching influence and power. He held rule over the chief priests, the elders, the scribes, and the business community. They were called Sadducees. They were the elite of the elite making up the majority of the top governing body, the Sanhedrin. While they were greatly outnumbered by the peasants, they were the ones who held all the power. Caiaphas stood at the top of this power pyramid.

He came to his post through the manipulation of his wealthy father-in-law, the former high priest, Annas, in 18 A.D. The high priest was appointed from Rome and Annas, who had loaned great amounts of money to certain Romans, was in a position to influence the selections.

Don't mistake Annas' intervention as Caiaphas' weakness. Caiaphas leaned on no one. He was a cunning man of great perception, possessing a seemingly inexhaustible supply of self-strength.

Caiaphas: I recall that it was the twelfth year of my being High Priest that word came to my office of some fiery preacher, dressed in sackcloth and ashes of all things, who was calling people to repentance. Furthermore he was claiming to be the forerunner of another who would be the Lord. Where do these people come from?

On the heels of this news came word that one Jesus, a carpenter's son out of Nazareth — and doesn't that figure? — was stirring up considerable interest among the people. I told my party members, "We've seen these passionate peasants before. Let's give them a little more rope and they'll likely hang themselves."

Later reports indicated that these men weren't hanging themselves, and the man Jesus was making real inroads into the lives of people. So I enlisted some of the scribes and Pharisees, explaining to them that the best way to apprehend him was to attend his gatherings and trip him up — expose him — by asking trick questions. Well, they did, but their traps never caught him. In fact they often came off second best in this battle of wits, and the numbers attending his teaching kept growing. He was a wily one.

So I had my people intensify their watching. We kept waiting for him to make some slip, to be caught in a petty infraction of the law, that we might discredit him. Several abortive attempts were made to arrest him. Yet his influence grew. Can't the people see through these self-appointed authorities?

Narrator: Caiaphas began to counsel regularly with the chief priests as to what they could do to end this man's disturbing, upsetting ministry. Caiaphas and others of the elite Sadducees had much to lose. Please understand that if there was some kind of religious upheaval in Israel, the Romans, who had lost both lives and money in earlier clashes, would strip the high priest and the Sadducees of their power. Caiaphas' great wealth and power depended upon continuing a good relationship with Rome. In turn, if he kept things under control, he was permitted to do as he wished.

About this time some of the Pharisees and priests heard that Jesus had been called to Bethany because his friend Lazarus had died. Trailing along with Jesus' party, they walked into the most amazing event of their lives — the raising of Lazarus from the dead. Greatly troubled that such power existed in one outside their group, they quickly returned to Jerusalem to report to Caiaphas and the Sanhedrin.

Caiaphas: "What are we going to do?" they cried. "This man performs many signs — we saw him raise Lazarus from the dead! — and he is steadily winning the people. Soon Rome will be inquiring of him, and if they have to intervene in a religious dispute again, our place may be taken away."

Well, I had given this some thought, and I knew I would need to speak with force if I was going to keep these twittering birds in line. "You know nothing at all," I told them. "You do not understand that it is better for you to have one man die for the people, than to have the whole nation destroyed" (John 11:49-50).

A high priest could never say that a man should be murdered, but he could slyly suggest that one man should die if it meant saving the blood of the people. It is far better that one man die than the whole nation, isn't it? Of course. So we laid our plans to bring him to death — for the good of the people, of course.

On the night we had arranged with Judas to have Jesus arrested, I called for a meeting of the Sanhedrin, so that we might immediately bring him to trial and find him guilty.

Narrator: Caiaphas didn't tell you that this trial was a farce. You need to know that it was illegal to hold a murder trial at night, and this one was undertaken late at night. The witnesses disagreed among themselves; this was a signal to end the trial and acquit the defendant, but that was ignored. The witnesses couldn't present anything for which he was guilty, let alone something that would condemn him to death.

Finally two men reported that they had heard Jesus brag that he could destroy the Temple and build it again in three days.

Caiaphas: This is what I had been waiting for. I left my seat as Judge, pushed the prosecutor aside, glared at this Jesus who had been silent throughout the trial, and shouted: "Have you no answer? What is it these men testify against you?" But he didn't reply. So I called upon the most solemn oath known to Hebrew life, the famous oath of testimony. "I put you under oath before the living God, tell us if you are the Messiah, the Son of God" (Matthew 26:62-64).

Jesus, so forced, replied, "You have said so."

Immediately I tore my robes, the symbol that blasphemy had been uttered. Raising my voice to a screaming pitch, I railed at the jurors: "Why do we still need witnesses? What is your verdict?"

41

Do you know what they said? "He deserves death." Of course (Matthew 26:65, 66).

Narrator: Caiaphas didn't tell you it was illegal for the high priest to invite or force a prisoner to convict himself. Nor was it within the law for the judge to leave the bench and take over the role of prosecutor. Nor did it bother Caiaphas and the Sanhedrin that while they found Jesus guilty of blasphemy, they presented him to Pilate guilty of treason.

Caiaphas: Before the trial in front of Pilate we had to work feverishly to use every means at our disposal to incite the people against Jesus. The crowds were very large due to the Passover, which meant that many of these strangers had not heard of Jesus. Playing on their loyalty to the faith, we told them that this Jesus had set out to destroy their faith and place himself above it. With such deep emotions stirred it was easy to manipulate uncritical minds to shout, "Crucify him! Crucify him!" So we won the day.

Perhaps you're taken aback by my straightforward speech? Well, I learned that if you are going to take power into your hands, then you need to be sure that all things are within your hands. If you can control things by speaking politely, then do it. But if tact and diplomacy don't lead you to your goals, then don't shy away from private confrontations where things are said bluntly and where blood might pockmark the conversation. It's when you go nose-to-nose that misunderstandings get cleared up. And I always reminded my adversary who was in charge. Once we all understood what was to be done, then we could return to polite pleasantries again. Our faith didn't come easily for us; we struggled over countless generations to preserve its meaning and practice. I was ready to pay the price. Yes, I lived well. I had a large home, servants, and modest wealth, but that wasn't what prompted my actions. No, it was the protection of the truth that gave shape to my days. This Jesus thought he had the truth, but the big difference between us was he didn't know how to handle power.

Narrator: Caiaphas, and those who preceded him in his office, once were open to the truth. They were daring in their pursuit of it. Slowly they gathered to themselves power, security, and the influence that attends the emergence of truth. It is a very heady wine.

When the crowds shouted for Jesus' death, Caiaphas had completed a very difficult and complex task — securing his power. Indeed he had won the day. He won other days as well. Twice he was the judge in trials of Peter and John. He presided when Stephen was found guilty. He was the one who commissioned Saul (Paul) to persecute the Christians in Damascus. He was in control.

However, not long after these events, in 37 A.D, he was removed from office. Rome, he was reminded, still called the shots. Within forty years the particular point of view he represented in Judaism was stripped of all influence. His group, the Sadducees, went into oblivion.

Strangely enough 2,000 years later, we refer to Jesus, the inept one according to Caiaphas, as "The King of Kings."

Pilate

Narrator: Pontius Pilate was a black-and-white-sighted man living in a world of many colors and shades of colors. He was a by-the-book man governing a by-the-book people; unfortunately their books had little in common. He was literal, to the point of being stubborn and rash. Those who peopled his province, however, were poetic, emotional, scheming, and skilled at playing the waiting game.

It has been speculated that the name Pontius derived from his fighting for Rome in Pontius, an area located in the Black Sea region. It has been more reasonably argued that Pontius was his family name, that he grew up in Rome, underwent diplomatic training, and climbed the administrative ladder until he was assigned to be the Governor of Judea. Yet, something about his blunt, forceful way of entering into most situations suggests some kind of military background. He was short of tact, long on show of strength.

When he first entered Jerusalem after his appointment by the Emperor, he was accompanied by Roman soldiers bearing banners, which bore the likeness of the emperor on the top of their staffs. That image was blasphemous to the Jews. There was only one deity to be recognized in their holy city, the God of Father Abraham.

Even though an agreement had been reached between Rome and Israel that *no* image of the Roman deity should appear in Jerusalem, Pilate took matters into his own hands and brought it in anyway. The Jews immediately protested, but Pilate refused to back down.

When Pilate and his entourage went to his home in Caesarea, thousands of protestors followed him, surrounding his home, dogging his every move, shrieking their unhappiness. Finally after four or five days he sent word to them that he would meet with them in the arena. What he didn't tell them was that his soldiers would surround the Jews once they were assembled. When gathered he announced that he would not back down from using the image and if they continued to harass him they would be killed. Then he gave them the order to return to Jerusalem immediately. But they didn't leave. Rather they knelt on the ground, bared their necks, and invited the soldiers to strike them. Not even hard-boiled Pilate could give the order to slay these defenseless rabble-rousers. Pilate, humiliated, ordered the images to be removed.

Pilate: I never did understand these people. They just didn't see how things were. We were the conquerors. We were the ones in charge, but they continued to act as if they could have their own way. Worse yet, Rome went along with their silliness. You have to give Judea a little more rope than some provinces, Rome counseled me, or they'll make your life miserable. Anyway we want to be just and fair conquerors and have our provinces think of us as friends. What poppycock!

Did you know that Jerusalem had no water system when I came? So I built an aqueduct, starting near Bethlehem. Since I found no money to fund the project, I took it from the Temple treasury. Then came such a barrage of complaining, as though I was doing something wrong! If they wouldn't use that money for something like this, by Caesar, I would. Rome didn't like my decision either.

I guess you're here to hear me talk about this man Jesus. Well, it was the Jews once again wanting their own way, goaded by the High Priest, Caiaphas. This time they wanted a teacher, healer, holy something or other put on trial because he was stirring up the people in their thinking. Okay, I said, this is some more of this religious arguing you people are always getting into. Well, I have nothing to do with that, so see to it yourselves. Anyway, I never did get all their babbling straightened out. There was no sense to it. It was yippity-yip this and yippity-yip that. So I had turned to walk away when Caiaphas shouted, "We are not permitted to put any one to death!" (John 18:31b).

Narrator: That stopped Pilate in his tracks. The Jewish governing body, the Sanhedrin, led by Caiaphas, had broad and pervasive powers, but they couldn't condemn someone to death. Such an order would require Pilate's signature. When he turned back to face the assembly and asked why the death penalty, they replied: "We have found this man perverting our nation, forbidding us to pay taxes to the Emperor and saying that he himself is the Messiah, a king" (Luke 23:2).

Pausing for a few moments, Pilate turned to an aide and asked him to bring Jesus inside.

Pilate: I could tell as soon as I had laid eyes on him that this was no insurrectionist. He was quiet and though he had been obviously roughed-up, there was no fire or defiance in his eyes. In fact, I didn't know what to make of him. He just stood there. So I asked him, "Are you the king of the Jews?" And he answered, "You say so" (Luke 23:3). "Don't you hear what their accusations are?" But he gave no reply. Nothing. He didn't show anger or fear. Nor did he seem withdrawn or sullen. He was simply silent. He was, what would you say, composed — that's it, composed. I can tell you I don't understand someone like that, but I had to admire him. That's strength. He was no ordinary man.

Now let me tell you something. I knew what Caiaphas and the Sanhedrin were up to. This Jesus, I figured, was getting into their territory. He was drawing crowds and, according to my soldiers, he was even healing people. If there was one thing that Caiaphas didn't want, it was competition. He had a good deal, he was the in-charge person next to me, and the Temple tax certainly gave him a good income. My guess is that he would have killed this Jesus in a minute, but he couldn't because the law forced him to come to me. He couldn't say to me, "I have someone getting in my way and I'd like to have him taken care of." So he presented to me the idea of treason: this man is setting himself up to be king. Well, I returned to Caiaphas and his henchmen — pardon me — the Sanhedrin and told them, "I find no case against him" (John 19:40). Then you should have heard them.

Narrator: What Pilate heard was another recital of the charges, many voices speaking at once making it impossible to follow anyone's line of thought very long. When he heard them say that Jesus stirred up the people in Judea and Galilee, and when he further learned that Jesus was a Galilean, he sent him to Herod, for Galilee was in Herod's jurisdiction. How he hoped this would end the matter! Dealing with these people on religious matters was the bane of his existence. As fate would have it — or was there another force at work? — Herod found no reason to deal with him and returned him to Pilate, but not before his soldiers had abused and mocked Jesus, striking and belittling a man who didn't retaliate.

Pilate: At this time of year we would free one man from prison, of the people's choosing. Remembering that I should negotiate with these people as Rome wanted, why not offer them Jesus as that man? They were way ahead of me. At my offer of Jesus, they countered with Barabbas, a real insurrectionist, to be set free. I couldn't believe it. Several times we went back and forth, but they were well prepared and organized and kept calling for Barabbas' release. "But what about this man?" I asked them as I gestured toward Jesus. And they simply cried, "Crucify, crucify him" (Luke 23:21).

Then my wife sent me a message in the midst of all this contention that she had had a dream about this innocent man and I should have nothing to do with him. Oh, great!

Once again I engaged this Jesus in private conversation and pointed out that I had the power of choosing life or death for him.

He replied, "You would have no power over me unless it had been given you from above" (John 19:11).

Above? Above? Is that where his kingdom is? He told me it wasn't from here. "If it was," he said, "my followers would be fighting to set me free." So where is it above? On a mountain? In the sky? With the gods of Rome?

Well, I couldn't get into that mystery. I had to get something nailed down so I could face Caiaphas. I put it to him that he must be a king then.

And he replied, "You say that I am a king. For this I was born, and for this I came into the world, to testify to the truth. Everyone who belongs to the truth listens to my voice" (John 18:37, 38).

"What is the truth?" I asked him. Why do these people talk in circles? Why does "yes" end up sounding like "no" and "no" sounding like "yes"? If he would have just played along with me, we could have set Caiaphas and the Sanhedrin back on their heels.

Narrator: Pilate again reported to the priests that he could not find Jesus guilty as charged. He announced that he would simply have him flogged and released. Screaming voices immediately united and rolled over him, "Crucify him, crucify him," like seventy-foot waves beating on a foundering ship. Pilate stood in defiance attempting to stare the crowd down. He knew their strategy. He knew the power move they were employing, but he couldn't think of a counter-strategy, except to be obstinate. Who knows, he might have won in the battle between shouts and stares, save for one piercing voice that rose above the clatter, "If you release this man you are no friend of the Emperor. Everyone who claims to be king sets himself against the Emperor" (John 19:12).

Pilate: That was their ultimate weapon. If I didn't go along with their madness, they'd get a message to Rome that I had failed to achieve an agreement again and I'd not only been insensitive, but released a man who was clearly Caesar's enemy. I couldn't defend myself, the fact was I was on probation because of earlier mishaps. I knew they would have a better reception in Rome than I. I had failed Rome too often. I was vulnerable. I couldn't risk the challenge. So they played their trump card and I had no choice but to go along. I ordered Jesus flogged as was required, and handed him over to be crucified.

I also ordered a basin of water and washed my hands, shouting to the crowd, "I am innocent of this man's blood, see to it yourselves" (Matthew 27:24c). They laughed as they said, "[Let it] be on us." They had won and that's all they cared about. Winning is everything, isn't it?

Underneath I was so angry to have been out-maneuvered, to be made a victim of my past. I searched for a way to strike back. I ordered the sign, "Jesus of Nazareth the King of the Jews" (John 19:19), to be put on the cross. When the Jews objected, wanting me to change the wording, I yelled at them, "What I have written, I have written" (John 19:22). Then they came to me saying they needed to bury Jesus before sundown, or the celebration of the Passover would be sullied or delayed. I sent word to have a centurion make sure he was dead before they removed him from the cross. They weren't going to bury him alive behind my back. The priests later came to me wanting my soldiers to seal the tomb. They were fearful that someone might steal his body, and then Jesus' people could claim he had risen from the dead, as he claimed he would. Well, now, I told them, that's your worry. See to it yourselves. Of all the nerve.

Narrator: That Pilate didn't anticipate the threat of being reported to Rome, in part reveals that he didn't see his blunders as his blunders, but as Rome's bleeding heart "just and fair" policy. In fact, his military-mindedness continued on past the trial of Jesus.

There was a religious disruption in a Samaritan village. His quick assessment of the situation convinced him it was a revolt against Roman rule. His troops massacred all the villagers. That heinous, unwarranted action marked the end of his days as Governor. Emperor Vitellis removed him from office.

Addendum: His wife, Claudia Procula, who warned Pilate not to get involved with Jesus, had a maid who was one of Jesus' followers. Later, Claudia was canonized by the Greek Orthodox Church for becoming a follower of Jesus. She was a granddaughter of Emperor Augustus and may have played a role in Pilate's being appointed to Judea.

What happened to Pilate? Some accounts say he was tried in Rome and imprisoned. Others report he was beheaded by Nero, or committed suicide when he knew he was to be beheaded. His body, or maybe it was just his head, was buried on Mount Pilatus above Lake Lucerne in Switzerland, casting an eerie spell over that place.

One researcher reported that the Abyssinian Church made Pilate a saint on the rather sparse evidence that he sought Jesus' forgiveness just before his death. We may suspect that this is the wishful thinking of early Christians who couldn't imagine anyone being thrust so intimately into the Savior's life without becoming a believer.

Nicodemus and
Joseph of Arimethea

Narrator: Two of the lesser players in the account of Jesus' death are Nicodemus and Joseph of Arimethea. They are best known as the cautious and secret converts. Yet these minor characters in the great drama of Jesus Christ's last hours, give rise to hope for all of us who at some critical juncture proved to be less than heroes. Joseph and Nicodemus didn't make public their confession until late in the afternoon of Jesus' crucifixion. Even then it was an unusual confession, caught only by a sensitive ear, or a perceptive eye. It may well have been that they were so skittish because as members of the Sanhedrin they were expected to remain true to the traditional faith.

Nicodemus actually sought out Jesus sometime before the crucifixion in the dark of night. Perhaps it was in the Garden of Gethsemane where Jesus often went to pray. He wanted to talk about the haunting matter of our intimacy with God, for he sensed that Jesus was of God.

Joseph of Arimethea, however, doesn't enter the Gospel accounts until Jesus had died on the cross and needed to be buried. Even so, we can construct a story that reliably puts him as an unobtrusive observer of Jesus many days and months before the events on Golgotha's hill.

It was in that gruesome place that they both emerged from the shadows of their closeted faith to provide the Master a dignified and proper burial. Maybe their act was "too little, too late," but it took courage and we honor them for that.

Nicodemus: I went to see Jesus at night for obvious reasons. It would have been risky in daytime, for I am a Pharisee and a member of the Sanhedrin. I didn't want people taking notice of my interest in this teacher, for he was considered to be a maverick and treasonous. Being seen with him could damage my position in the Jewish community.

Perhaps Jesus was a little nervous too, for it might have been damaging for him to be seen with the likes of me. I began telling him how much I admired his teaching and that surely he must be of God. His reply was somewhat blunt, for he insisted that only those who were born from above would have knowledge of who is of God's Kingdom. Then he launched into a description of the necessity of being born again, which was a confusing topic to me. To clarify, he said it was necessary to be born a second time of the spirit. I must have looked puzzled, for he went on to explain that it is something like the wind which we can't see coming or going and yet we know that it is real.

"Yes, yes," I murmured, but when I proved at last to be a dense student, he chastised me with, "Are you a teacher of Israel, and yet you do not understand these things?" (John 3:10).

That teacher knew something I wanted to know. While his teaching cut across what I believed, creating an inner chaos, I couldn't turn away from him.

Joseph of Arimethea: While I don't appear in the New Testament accounts until the afternoon of Jesus' death, I had been following his ministry for some time. As a Pharisee, under the direction of the High Priest, I took my turn listening and spying on him. While I remained faithful to my duties and allegiance to the Sanhedrin, I was also paying close attention to Jesus' teachings, healings, and especially the relationships he established with his disciples and the crowds. Even his off-hand remarks were insightful.

He was beautiful to watch. He was perceptive, loving, confrontational — especially with us Pharisees — and aware. He was always aware. You remember the occasion when in the midst of a crowd he stated that someone had touched him. Those with him said, "Well, yes, but there are so many about you." Someone had touched him and he felt power leave his body. Most assuredly someone had touched him, someone wanting and needing to be healed. He wasn't angry, defensive, or suspicious; he simply wanted to confirm what had happened and then bless the one who had been healed. He was so aware.

Narrator: Joseph and Nicodemus were both members of the Sanhedrin, the top religious governing body of Israel. Undoubtedly they were wealthy and influential, yet were faulted for not being more courageous in their defense of Jesus. William Barclay, the biblical scholar, uses them to illustrate what it is to fail witnessing to the faith. Why didn't they become adherents as did the disciples? However, the disciples weren't all that courageous in facing the enemy either.

Joseph and Nicodemus kept their growing interest under wraps, all the while listening and learning more. Eventually they cared for this teacher and stood up for him while most of the disciples clung to the shadows.

Nicodemus: The High Priest once sent the temple police to arrest Jesus, but when they came to where he was and began listening, they became so moved they couldn't arrest him. When they returned they were criticized for their failure. The priests had already judged Jesus, you see, and didn't need any other evidence.

I pointed out on the occasion that the law makes it possible for every person to be given the opportunity to defend and explain himself. Jesus, it became clear, was not to be given that opportunity, so I was immediately suspect. "Are you a Galilean too?" I was asked. Furthermore, they reminded me, there was to be no prophet to come out of Galilee. In other words, we've already made up our minds and if you know what's good for you, you'll go along. I must confess I went along. Once prejudice is set into motion nothing, seemingly, will sidetrack or stop it.

Joseph: When the High Priest, Caiaphas, had determined the outcome of Jesus' trial before the Sanhedrin had ever assembled, there were no wiser minds powerful enough to change the outcome. I did not vote "yes" as did all the others, for when I saw what was going to happen, I left the trial. I couldn't bear to watch it. No, I didn't speak up. I looked down at my feet, so I wouldn't see Jesus as I left. I've regretted my cowardice many times.

I stayed in Jerusalem however, and the next afternoon I was standing just a short way from the cross. My conscience said this was the least I could do. As the day wore on I became aware that another crisis was mounting. The family of Jesus, I discovered through inquiry, didn't have a grave to bury him, nor did they have the money necessary to buy one. Which meant Jesus would possibly be left on the cross, or laid on the ground. Even if he did have a tomb, what if he didn't die in time to allow the burial before sundown — the beginning of Passover? Then it became clear what I could do. I had a newly hewn-out tomb nearby; Jesus could be buried there. So I hurried into the city and bought linen in which the corpse could be wrapped. Then I ran to Pilate's headquarters to seek his permission for Jesus' body to be released to me for burial.

He recognized me from the Sanhedrin and, not fully trusting that my intentions were honorable, dispatched a soldier to confirm that the King of the Jews was indeed dead before granting his approval. I didn't tell Pilate that Jesus was still alive when I last saw him. He waited and waited and at last the soldier returned and, thank God, he said that the King of the Jews was dead. Well, you understand I didn't want him dead, but if we were to bury him by sundown we needed ... oh, you understand.

*   *   *   *   *

Joseph: All right, men, you'll need to place the ladders on the cross arms as best you can. Remember, you'll need to support his body, or he'll come crashing down. Nicodemus, what brings you here?

Nicodemus: (*Out of breath*) ... I've brought ... some myrrh and aloes ... about 100 pounds, not enough really ... put the bag down there, son ... that's enough for now.

Joseph: Bless you, Nicodemus, you did what I couldn't. Catch your breath, then please give us a hand with Jesus. Men, put the block closer to his hand, set the lever to lift the nail. It'll take more force. It's coming. Lift up on his shoulders. Good, good. Hold his body! (*Turns to the crowd*) We can use some more hands here.

Nicodemus: Let me assist with the feet. We'll need a bigger block. Yes, that's it, now pry. Push harder. Reposition the block. Now once more. I'm sorry, my woman, can't you see that this is a very difficult task and you'll only be in the way?

Mary Magdalene: He is my master. I've followed him for years, I must help him down. And I'm strong, truly I'm strong.

Joseph: We can't hold his weight much longer.

Nicodemus: Please, woman, step aside until we free his feet. More pressure on the bar; now it's out! Hold his body; he's falling.

Mary Magdalene: Oh, Master, let me cradle you in my arms. It's me, Mary. It's not right that you should die — but you knew, didn't you — and you said, "Forgive them." How like you.

Joseph: I'm very sorry, woman.

Mary Magdalene: Mary.

Joseph: Mary. We need to prepare his body for burial in great haste lest we lose the race with the sun.

Mary Magdalene: I understand and I will help.

Joseph: Lay out the linen, men. Over here next to his body.

Mary Magdalene: Allow me to wash his face.

Nicodemus: Helpers, permit me to show you how to place the spices, then move quickly.

Joseph: Yes, that's how to wrap his body, keep busy there with the aloes. That's it, roll him over. More spices.

Mary Magdalene: Wait, wait. The blood is matted in his hair. If only I had warm water. Oh, Master, when will you come back? You said you would. When may we look for you? You are the resurrection.

Nicodemus: You truly believe he will return, don't you, Mary?

Mary Magdalene: With all my heart.

Nicodemus: But what if he doesn't?

Mary Magdalene: Oh, but he will.

Joseph: Mary, I would be greatly comforted if I could believe as you.

Mary Magdalene: You can.

Nicodemus: It is not easy for us. Maybe we know too many things.

Mary Magdalene: Then you need to know *him* more. Come join our band of believers.

Joseph: Yes, perhaps. But right now we need to take him to the tomb. It's not that far away. In fact, look where I'm pointing. It's the new tomb.

Nicodemus: Men, let us get on both sides of his body. Stand as close to each other as you can. Now squat down and reach under to find the hands of the man across from you. Now, all together, lift! Good. Well done, now move.

Narrator: Joseph, Nicodemus, and their men carried Jesus to the tomb without mishap, and as carefully as they could they laid his body to rest. They placed a white napkin on his face. Finally, Joseph and several others heaved a large stone in front of the door to the tomb. This would keep at bay any robbers or predatory animals. They beat the setting sun by minutes and, brushing off their clothes as best they could, they hurried into town to prepare for the feast. The hidden converts at last stepped out into the remaining light of that crucial day.

Mary and the other women stood at a distance and planned to bring more spices on the first day of the week to complete the burial preparations for their Master. For a final moment they stood shivering in the growing darkness while silence engulfed the wretched place of the skull.

Addendum: You might be wondering what happened to our two characters, Nicodemus and Joseph, following Jesus' death.

Nicodemus
Legend has it that he was baptized into the faith by Peter and John. For some reason he was banished from Jerusalem during the Jewish uprising against Stephen. Turncoats make people uneasy. It is not possible to know the full nature of his discipleship, though many traditions credit him with becoming a faithful follower of Jesus. An apocryphal writing is credited to Nicodemus, which is simply titled, *The Gospel of Nicodemus*.

Joseph of Arimethea
He came from Ramlah, near Lydda on the coastal plain southwest of Jerusalem. According to *The Gospel of Nicodemus*, he helped found the first Christian community in Lydda. More romantic is the legend of Joseph making a voyage to England and taking with him the chalice, or Holy Grail, used at the Last Supper. It became the object of swashbuckling adventures as the colorful and courageous knights of England went in search of it. Much was made of this by the historian William of Malmesbury in the twelfth century.

Dialogue 9

Mary, Mother of Jesus

Narrator: Mary and her devout parents may have once lived in Jerusalem, but while Mary was quite young they moved to Nazareth. There it was that her family met Joseph's family and eventually it was accomplished that Mary was betrothed to Joseph. Mary was likely a teenager, perhaps as young as fourteen or fifteen. Joseph, it was estimated, was in his late twenties. During the year of their betrothal — a formal and lasting arrangement that could not be broken except by divorce — the angel Gabriel came to Mary with the wonderful news that the Lord God wanted her to give birth to his son, the Messiah. With a calmness and steadiness that typifies someone much older, Mary replied, "Here am I, the servant of the Lord; let it be according to your word" (Luke 1:38).

Well, of course, she wondered how all this would take place, as she pointed out to Gabriel, "I am a virgin" (Luke 1:34). However, when she was told that the Holy Spirit would come over her — overshadow her — she was fully accepting of the explanation.

Joseph, at first, was not nearly so accepting of this turn of events. He planned to divorce Mary, albeit quietly, thinking this would be less traumatic for her. Then Joseph was visited in a dream by an angel who informed him that Mary's child was to be of the Holy Spirit and he should not hesitate to marry her. Indeed he was further instructed to name the child Jesus, for he would save his people from all their sins. When Joseph awoke from his dream he did exactly what he had been told. We may wonder if the people who were acquainted with Joseph thought him to be foolish. Faithfulness can look like foolishness to an outsider.

Why, of all the maidens of Israel, was a teenage Mary selected to give birth to the Messiah? We can speculate that the choice was made taking into account her family heritage, physical stock, emotional maturity, and sympathetic husband-to-be. However, when we look back across her life we see two qualities that appear over and over again — she was believing and obedient.

Mary: Believe me, I felt so thrilled to be selected to bear God's Son. Could any other honor be greater? Even so, I was overwhelmed by my new responsibility, and it didn't help that Joseph was a little strange to me at first. Even after he understood, there were still all the whispers within our families and the village. It was hard to stay composed.

So I was greatly relieved when it became possible for me to visit Elizabeth. I've always loved Elizabeth. Being with her was not only a break from the tensions at home, but an affirmation of what I had been asked to do. She was also pregnant and the babe within her jumped for joy at my arrival, for her son, you see, would be the forerunner of my son. I could scarcely believe it. Elizabeth didn't just understand the role I was to play, she was overjoyed for me and also for herself.

Just when I needed assurance and support I got it in such quantities I couldn't contain it all. In fact, I stayed with her three months and I never forgot that respite. Many times in later years I would return in my memory to experience the high moments of those days when praise came spontaneously to my lips.

> *My soul magnifies the Lord.*
> *And my spirit rejoices in God my Savior*
> *For he has looked with favor on*
> *The lowliness of his servant.*
>
> *Surely, from now on all*
> *Generations will call me blessed;*
> *For the Mighty One has done great things for me,*
> *Holy is his name.*
> — Luke 1:46-49

Narrator: It might cross our minds to think that she was too young to become the mother of God's son. It all seems so simplistic and innocent. If we had known of the event before it took place, we might have prayed, "God, are you sure you want to do this?

Shouldn't he be born in a more reliable environment, with an older and experienced mother? This is untried and risky." Now that we are on this side of the event, we readily admit that young family, in that crude barn, with that beautiful baby has captivated our hearts.

Mary: Soon after I returned to Nazareth, Joseph and I began a trip to Bethlehem. We had to register there since we were of the family of David. Joseph did everything he could to ease the agony of the journey, but I was so miserable on the back of that plodding donkey that I didn't fully appreciate his efforts. It seemed to me that whatever he did wasn't nearly enough. Somehow we muddled through the nightmare of seeking shelter when I was already having birth pains. I remember offers of help, clean straw, an older woman, firm counsel, a pale-faced Joseph, and pain and pain. Then finally relief, a squalling baby, and blessed sleep.

Some rough and ready shepherds stopped by to report excitedly on angels singing to them in the hills and instructing them to come to our stable. Many days later some exquisitely dressed men from the East brought extravagant gifts and words of such magnitude that I couldn't comprehend. Yet what words I did understand I treasured and pondered them in my heart.

Narrator: Eight days after Jesus' birth, Joseph and Mary made the trip to Jerusalem for their son's circumcision and Mary's rites of purification. At the temple they met a devout and righteous man, Simeon, chosen by the Holy Spirit, who was aware of the unique role the young infant would play in the life of Israel. He also sounded what would become a death knell, when he said to Mary "... and a sword will pierce your own soul too" (Luke 2:35). Sometimes a hundred sentences may be spoken, but one will fasten itself in our memory and any effort to erase it will meet with failure.

After returning to Bethlehem, Joseph was warned again by an angel in a dream to move his family to Egypt quickly for Herod was determined to kill his son. Immediately he sprang into action to protect his family. Mary coped with being a new mother on-the-run in a strange land. We can only guess that she met each challenge as she met all the other challenges in her life. The young family had been in Egypt for two years when once more an angel informed Joseph that Herod had died and they were to go home. They settled in Nazareth, where Joseph began to ply his carpenter's trade.

Mary and Joseph had four more sons, James, Joseph, Judas, and Simon, and some daughters (Matthew 13:55-56). About thirteen years after returning to Nazareth, Joseph died. Mary then became a single parent depending on her oldest son, a very young teenager, to be a breadwinner.

Mary: In the year that Jesus was twelve, Joseph and I determined to take him to Jerusalem during the Feast of the Passover. In fact, all those of our village attending the feast decided to travel together. We did this for reasons of safety, and it was also a great opportunity to visit with friends and extended family. Our pace was slow due to the short legs of our young ones and the uncertain legs of our older ones. That meant that the older children could be playing at the front, middle, or back of our village's procession.

It was on the return trip — a full day out, in fact — that Joseph and I realized that neither of us had seen Jesus. Rather frantically we searched through all our friends and family and finally realized that he must still be back in Jerusalem. Leaving the other children with relatives, the two of us retraced our steps. Back in Jerusalem, after asking and searching for three days, we finally found him in the Temple talking to the teachers. They were amazed at his learning, but I was beside myself with worry, so I shouted at him, "Child, why have you treated us like this? Look, your father and I have been searching for you in great anxiety." And his response set us back on our heels: "Why were you searching for me? Did you not know that I must be in my Father's house?" (Luke 2:48-50). We were stunned by his apparent impudence. Obviously we didn't fully understand what he meant. However, we wasted no time in heading back to Nazareth and I kept his words etched in my memory.

Narrator: This event was the beginning of Jesus' pulling away from his parents. Not that he was rebelling against them — rather he was starting to travel his own unique road in response to his heavenly Father.

Perhaps Jesus' seemingly curt response, "Did you not know that I must be in my Father's house?" (Luke 2:49) might today sound like, "You know what my role on earth is to be. So why are you angry with me?"

The uniqueness of Jesus as teacher, healer, and speaker of truth was now coming to the fore.

Mary: The days, months, and years following Joseph's death, I confess, are indistinct — a continuous blur of family, work, and religious activities. I had the care of seven children, the oldest of whom was mastering his father's trade. I gave him the support I could, but I knew little about carpentry. His commitment to his heavenly Father, however, never diminished; it grew and I believe mine grew also. When Jesus' brothers were old enough to practice their father's trade, Jesus made a decision to begin his public teaching. I followed him as best I could, watching and listening in hope and sometimes in fear.

One day I attended a wedding in Cana, here in Galilee. Jesus and some of his friends had been invited also. When the wine ran out, I turned to Jesus and apprised him of the situation. I knew he was capable of handling the moment. He surprised me with his answer: "Woman, what concern is that to you and to me? My hour has not yet come" (John 2:3-5). Startled, but wanting to appear as if everything was going smoothly, I turned to the servants and said, "Do whatever he tells you." This was yet another time when I only dimly understood what he was saying, but I was certain he would not let the wedding party down — and he didn't. I ran his words through my mind many times that day. My son had gone someplace in his faith where I had never gone and where I'd never completely follow.

Narrator: The separation Mary experienced in her relationship to Jesus was to increase. And it wasn't only Mary who felt the growing breach. When Jesus came to his hometown to teach, his friends and neighbors were astounded. "Is this the carpenter's son? Is not his mother called Mary? And are not his brothers James and Joseph and Simon and Judas? And are not all his sisters with us? Where then did this man get all this?" (Matthew 13:55, 56).

When the same response to his teachings happened again, word came to Mary and Jesus' brothers that "he was going out of his mind" (Mark 3:21). So Mary and Jesus' brothers came for him, expecting to take him home. When Jesus was told his mother and brothers were calling for him, he startled his listeners by saying, "Who are my mother and my brothers?" Then looking at those sitting around him he said, "Here are my mother and brothers." Then he explained, "Whoever does the will of God is my brother and sister and mother" (Mark 3:31-35).

On another occasion when Jesus was teaching, a woman cried out to him, "Blessed is the womb that bore you and the breasts that nursed you!" But he countered, "Blessed rather are those who hear the word of God and obey it!" (Luke 11:27-28).

We can guess that any mother would be hurt by these seemingly blunt pronouncements. A lesser mother might have said, "If that's the way he feels, he can go his own way, until he comes to his senses."

Mary had stored many things in her heart from the fateful day that the angel Gabriel had visited her. She could still hear his words spoken three decades before. "Do not be afraid, Mary, for you have found favor with God ... you will conceive in your womb and bear a son, and you will name him Jesus ... he will be called the Son of the Most High ... He will reign over the house of Jacob forever ... of his kingdom there will be no end" (Luke 1:30-33).

Mary: John, the beloved disciple, and others tried to spare me from Jesus' trial and crucifixion. They were wanting to shield me and urged me to stay home, away from witnessing the grizzly business of men putting another man to death for the sake of preserving their own status in the community. But I could not stay away. My commitment to my God and to my son ran too deep.

The scene at the cross frightened me. Who were all these people? Why were they so angry? Why did some of them laugh, joke, and roll dice? Were the soldiers necessary? Why did my old neighbors avert their eyes? I huddled close to John, Mary Magdalene, and the other women.

All the while my son's body grew weaker and ashen gray and his voice became only a rasping whisper. He was in such agony and was dying. I thought surely, surely I would die too. My beloved firstborn suffering such torture. When he cried, "My God, my God, why have you forsaken me?" (Mark 15:34), my heart broke and I could not control my sobbing. Then he raised his anguished eyes and looked directly at me, "Woman, here is your son!" and looking at John whispered, "Here is your mother" (John 19:26, 27). While it tore me apart to hear these words, it was, in a strange way, a validation of my contribution to his life. As the eldest son, he was making provision for me, his mother. I had a unique place in his heart. Then, in great relief my son bowed his head one last time and said, "It is finished" (John 19:30).

I watched as men, not well known to me, assisted by Mary Magdalene, removed Jesus' body from the cross and prepared him for burial. My feet seemed rooted to the ground and I might have stood there indefinitely, but John tugged at my elbow, "Come, Mother," he said, "it is time to go." I went to the home of my newly-appointed son. It proved to be the most wearisome journey of my life.

Narrator: Many questions linger about the devoted life of Mary. Some come from her first-century life and some from later centuries when the Western Church added to or changed the nature of her life.

For example, why didn't Jesus place Mary in the care of one of his brothers? It is speculated that none of Jesus' brothers believed in him, until after the resurrection. So Jesus placed Mary under the care of his true family, in other words among those who believed. Why wasn't Mary more intimately involved in Jesus' burial? Always before she had stood by him, so why at this moment did she seem to be standing back, looking over the shoulders of others? By this time Mary was nearly fifty, an old woman in first-century Israel; physically she may have been very limited in

67

what she could do. Or to put it less elegantly, time had set her aside; she was no longer in charge.

Then how was she transformed from a loving, earthly mother, who seemed held by all the limitations that surround all other mothers, to become a God-like mother, one not only worthy of our adulation, but of our worship? How did she become one to whom people may pray, one who takes her place not far distant from the Father, Son, and Holy Spirit?

The Western, or as named later, the Roman Catholic Church, came to believe that Mary was of much more spiritual significance than the New Testament accounts would lead us to believe. This led to Mariolatry, which is the veneration or worship of Mary. Early this led to a denial of Mary having other children than Jesus. His brothers and sisters were explained away as stepbrothers and sisters, or perhaps as cousins. This emphasized that Mary was placed here on earth to give birth to the Christ Child and him alone. To further elevate her purity and in preparation for her unique role, Pope Pius IX, in December 1854, set forth the Immaculate Conception which said the virgin from the moment of her conception "was preserved from all stain of original sin." It almost sounds like Mary was no longer mortal.

Mary: The New Testament story contains none of these speculations of the Western Church. My story concludes with my going to John's home. But wait, that isn't all, for living with him I heard all about the resurrection; I heard the accounts of those who saw my son. I was present when that early fellowship met to praise God and sing. I can't tell you what a joy it was to know that my son had brought salvation to Israel, just as the angel had promised. But saving the best for last, I was able to be present on the day of my son's ascension into heaven. That was enough for me. I had kept the course. I now knew joy.

John, the Beloved Disciple

Narrator: John, sometimes described as Jesus' beloved disciple, never attained the prominence of Peter, or perhaps even that of Judas, with the millions of Christians across the centuries. While he offered a courageous and open witness to the faith, his enduring contribution was made as Jesus' confidant, a thoughtful advisor to the early Church — and most prominently — as the mind, if not the writer, of the Gospel of John, the Epistles of John 1, 2, and 3, and the book of Revelation.

His Gospel written for the Greek or Western mind is often cited by many modern-day Westerners as the Gospel of choice. Its thought patterns seem to mesh so easily with ours. While we may not have as sharp an image of John as we do of Peter, we highly value his written word.

John and his brother James were the sons of Zebedee, a well-established man of the fishing industry. In fact, John and James quite literally left their boats and net-mending to follow Jesus one day. We can imagine that Zebedee was dismayed that his sons "walked off the job" to follow an itinerate teacher with no discernible means of support. Their mother, however, took a keen interest in Jesus and busied herself to promote her sons' ranking with Jesus, a move that angered the other disciples. Even so, Jesus still included John and James with Peter as the men he wanted for his inner circle.

John: Almost from the beginning of our venture, Jesus selected Peter, my brother James, and me to witness a most unusual event. I often wondered why he chose us, but never quite found the appropriate time or the courage to ask him. Well, this day he took us up the mountain and he was transfigured — made luminous — before our very eyes, was visited by Elijah and Moses, and finally was blessed by a heavenly voice that said, "This is my son, the beloved, with whom I am well pleased, listen to him!" (Mark 9:2-8). We dropped to the ground in fear. How could we stand in the presence of such an event? Jesus saw that we were frightened and overwhelmed, so he encouraged, nay ordered, us to get up and not be afraid. We knew our Master to be unusual and unique, but we had no idea at this point of his standing with our Heavenly Father. Of course we wanted to tell others what we saw and heard, but he forbad us to tell anyone until after his resurrection. We could only guess that, for the time being, this event was just for the four of us. Did he want us to be certain that he was who he said he was? I wondered more than ever why I had been included in that intimate circle. What could I contribute? Believe me, I wanted to hold up my end responsibly.

Jesus also selected the three of us to go with him when he went to heal Simon's mother-in-law. Again he had us accompany him when he was invited to the synagogue leader's home to heal his daughter. The people there thought he had come too late. When he tried to allay their fears by saying the daughter was only asleep, they laughed. Jesus was not deterred in the least. He simply called to her, "Little girl, get up," and immediately she got up (Mark 5:41).

The Master was so confident and certain of who he was and what he could do.

One day he sat the three of us down to talk about "end times." Later it was Peter and I he chose to prepare a place for the Last Supper, and finally he selected all three of us to accompany him to the Garden of Gethsemane. While we stood by him on other occasions, that night we failed him. We didn't listen to his word; we literally fell asleep.

Narrator: John never spoke of Gethsemane; I think it shamed him deeply. He always thought of enemies as being outside himself. Therefore, why would Jesus need him to stay awake? Jesus was safe enough in the Garden. But Jesus' enemy was to emerge from within and would bring him to a moment of great sorrow. John would not know of this until it was too late.

He was, however, ready for the outside enemy. Once he saw a man casting out demons in Jesus' name. He thought he was usurping Jesus' power and would have stopped him, but Jesus intervened in the man's behalf.

Another time a Samaritan village did not welcome the disciples, so John asked Jesus if he should bring down fire to consume them. Jesus once more intervened. There was nothing very subtle about the way John wanted to handle a perceived enemy.

John was ambitious. Once John and James, called the "sons of thunder," came to Jesus and announced, "Teacher, we want you to do for us whatever we ask of you" (Mark 10:35-45). Prompted, perhaps by their mother's coaching, we find nothing delicate about their approach. Jesus was not ready to say, "Well, sure, men, whatever you want." Rather he wanted to know what it was they wanted. Perhaps we can admire their blunt honesty, "Grant us to sit, one at your right hand and one at your left, in your glory."

Startled, Jesus said, "You don't know what you're asking. Can you drink the cup I drink, or be baptized as I?"

Quite assured, they responded, "We are able" (Mark 10:37, 38).

Then Jesus concluded that they would drink the cup and be baptized as was he, but he informed them that the positions they sought were not his to give. The other disciples were angry at their brazen approach — their open attempt to become the greatest in the kingdom. Jesus then taught them the necessity of becoming a slave or a servant of all.

Perhaps John's last effort as a man-in-charge came on the night of Jesus' arrest in the Garden. Peter and an unidentified man followed Jesus and the soldiers to Caiaphas' mansion. That unknown man scholars have since concluded was John. John went right through Caiaphas' gate into the courtyard and no one questioned him. When he saw Peter standing outside, he arranged with the maid to allow him to come in. Was he known there? Did he have influence there?

Obviously John was not a simple man. It's not possible to wrap him up in a nice, neat package. However, as his life moved along, he became more focused and revealed a gentler John that resulted in his being called the beloved disciple.

John: I suppose you noticed that my name doesn't appear in the Gospel or in the letters that claim me as author. It seems a little strange to me, now, for as I look at your New Testament I see my name in the other Gospels, Acts, Galatians, and Revelation.

It was my intention to highlight Jesus as the Christ. I wanted no one to be in error. He was the Messiah, the Savior, the Risen One. He was the light and the Word of God. Therefore, I determined to keep myself out of view as much as possible. The most obvious way was to keep my name out of the manuscript. I didn't write down every word; my aides assisted me frequently. They insisted that I couldn't be totally omitted, for I played such a key role in the life of Christ and in the establishment of the Church. They are the ones who came up with the "beloved disciple" phrase to identify me in a hidden kind of way.

Now I'm glad that you know that Peter and I were the ones who arranged the details for the Last Supper, that Jesus selected me to care for his mother, and I'm especially pleased that you know that I beat Peter in our foot race to the empty tomb. He was so often out ahead of the rest of us, it felt good once to get the best of him. Following the resurrection, Jesus waited on the seashore one morning, looking for us who were coming in from fishing. I was the first one to recognize him in his resurrected body.

Narrator: That incident of John, so quickly recognizing Jesus at a distance, suggests how well he knew the Master. What was it that allowed John to identify him before the others? Was it Jesus' stance? Was it the sun picking up the unusual highlights of Jesus' hair? Or was the Master in a pose much like other men, but with that subtle difference that immediately informed John who he was? Two people separated as far as human is from divine, yet so close that they could trust each other's word without question. The Messiah and the fisherman. The upfront teacher and the behind-the-scenes thinker, the peacemaker and the competitor, the proclaimer and the believer.

John: Shortly after Jesus' ascension into heaven, Peter and I found ourselves thrust to the forefront, for Peter this was familiar territory.

Once it was familiar territory for me, but on this day it was a strange and forbidding place. You see, the two of us were on our way to the Temple to pray when we encountered a lame man who asked us for coins. Peter immediately explained that we had no silver or gold, but that we would gladly share with him what we did have. I gulped, what did Peter think we had — and why didn't he just pass by? There were always more maimed people begging than we had alms. Then Peter said, "In the name of Jesus Christ of Nazareth, stand up and walk" (Acts 3:6). Whereupon Peter took the man's hand and helped him to his feet, and almost instantly the man began to walk and leap. He made quite a stir, for people coming here every day remembered his former condition. Peter was so quick to take advantage of whatever opportunity presented itself. So when a crowd gathered to see what happened, Peter seized the moment to preach.

I must say Peter was forthright, but sometimes I wished he was a little more diplomatic. The authorities were upset about Peter's preaching and moved quickly to arrest us and put us in jail for the night. If only Peter would have toned down his message a little, "You rejected the holy and righteous one ... you killed the author of life." If only he had softened his accusations, "And now, friends, I know that you acted in ignorance, as did also your rulers" (Acts 3:14-17). Perhaps we could have gone unnoticed.

The next day we were brought before the rulers, scribes, elders, and even Annas and Caiaphas, the former and present high priests. We were questioned about the healing of the beggar: "By what power or by what name did you do this?" (Acts 4:17). Again Peter spoke plainly, very plainly. I dreaded to think of what might become of us. The authorities then dismissed us temporarily and huddled together. Finally they called us to them and ordered us not to speak in the name of Jesus again. Then, and I could hardly believe it, I found my voice accompanying Peter's. "Whether it is right in God's sight to listen to you rather than God, you must judge, for we cannot keep from speaking about what we have seen and heard" (Acts 4:19, 20). I was astounded at my wagging tongue. After threatening us again, they let us go. They might have beaten us, but they were put off by the people who had seen the healing who didn't want to see us imprisoned or harmed.

Narrator: Word came to these early Christians that some citizens of Samaria had become believers, so the community sent Peter and John to see if they were true believers. The two men had been elevated to high positions by their brethren. They met with the Samaritans and found them to be true believers indeed.

Later when Paul, who had been a persecutor of the Christians, was searching for approval that he might preach and witness to the faith, he met with various believers. But at last his "credentials" were established only after he was given the right hand of fellowship by none other than Peter, James, and John. Paul referred to them as "the acknowledged pillars." They were the new wave of leadership.

John: Soon our Christian community was engulfed with all kinds of challenges, such as spreading the word, caring for widows, raising money for the poor, creating an organization, establishing a moral code, handling of funds, assigning who was to preach and teach, where and when, etc. We almost drowned in a sea of details. In the meantime a more insidious enemy, Gnosticism, was emerging that could corrupt the very basic beliefs of our fellowship. I was alarmed that our faith could grow an offshoot that would threaten the main body of our faith. More importantly, we needed to tell the story of salvation so that it would make sense to the Greek world — the Gentiles. Finally we needed to make clear that Jesus was the Christ and make no mistake about it!

Narrator: To this day a debate continues as to the authorship of the Gospel of John, the epistles of John, and the book of Revelation, which is also attributed to him. Perhaps it's a moot point, for a number of scholars agree if John didn't literally write or dictate these words, then the person/persons who did were so imbued with his thought that their words truly represent John's beliefs.

The other Gospel writers wanted to set down the story of Jesus — an historical record. John's story of Jesus was also a record, but further it was a correction of a misbelief (Gnosticism) and a preparation for the future. He had set his sights on tomorrow and on the world beyond Israel. He wanted to set forth a proclamation of the faith that would endure in the midst of very different and unknown cultures. To this day his thought provides a steady hand as we attempt to understand how Jesus was both human and divine.

John: My brother James was the first martyr of that earliest Christian community. Some scholars have thought I was martyred. Others tell you I went to Ephesus and oversaw the work of the Western Church from that great city.

It is enough for me to know that you would read the books attributed to me, especially the Gospel account. I cannot tell you how excited, thrilled, scared, determined, hopeful, and assured we disciples felt in those three years we accompanied Jesus in Galilee and Judea. You see, we had life, truth, and love right in our midst. He was also the resurrection and the giver of eternal life. Could any journey in life be filled with more meaning and joy!

He still lives. Here. His power and hope have not diminished. It still is a matter of belief and faithfulness. The events that unfold will be different, but the inherent possibilities within them are still in his hands.

Scriptural References

Peter
Matthew: 4:18-22; 8:14-15; 10:1-4; 14:28-31; 16:13-20; 17:1-4, 24-27; 18:21-22; 19:27-30; 26:30-75
Mark: 3:13-19; 5:35-37; 8:27-33; 9:2-8; 10:24-31; 11:20-26; 13:1-8; 14:26-72; 16:6-8
Luke: 5:1-11; 6:12-16; 8:42b-48; 9:18-22, 28-33; 12:41; 18:25-30; 22:7-13, 28-62
John: 1:35-45; 6:66-71; 13:5-11, 21-26, 36-38; 18:10-27; 20:1-10; 21:1-23
Acts: 1:12-26; 2:14-42; 3:1-26; 4:1-22; 5:1-32; 8:14-24; 9:32-43; 10:5-48; 11:1-18; 12:1-9; 15:6-21
Galatians: 1:18; 2:4-16
1 Peter
2 Peter

Judas
Matthew: 10:1-4; 26:14-50; 27:3-10
Mark: 3:13-19; 14:10-11, 17-21, 43-46
Luke: 6:12-16; 22:3-6, 21-23, 47-51
John: 6:66-71; 12:1-8; 13:2, 21-30; 18:2-5
Acts: 1:15-19, 24-25

Barabbas
Matthew: 27:15-26
Mark: 15:6-15
Luke: 23:18-25
John: 18:38b-40

Simon of Cyrene
Matthew: 27:32
Mark: 15:21
Luke: 23:26
Acts: 13:1
Romans: 16:13

Mary Magdalene
Matthew: 27:55-61; 28:1-10
Mark: 15:40-47; 16:1-9
Luke: 8:1-3; 23:55—24:12
John: 19:25; 20:1-3, 10-18

Thomas
Matthew: 10:1-4
Mark: 3:13-19
Luke: 6:12-16
John: 11:11-16; 14:1-7; 20:24-29; 21:1-3f
Acts: 1:12-14

Caiaphas
Matthew: 26:3, 57-68
Mark: 14:53-65
Luke: 3:2
John: 11:49-53; 18:13, 19-24, 28
Acts: 4:5-21

Pilate
Matthew: 27:2-65
Mark: 15:1-45
Luke: 3:1; 13:1; 23:1-25, 50-52
John: 18:23-40; 19:1-38
Acts: 2:23; 3:13; 4:27; 13:28
1 Timothy: 6:13

Nicodemus
John: 3:1-10; 7:45-52; 19:38-42

Joseph of Arimethea
Matthew: 27:57-61
Mark: 14:64; 15:42-47
Luke: 23:50-56
John: 19:38

Mary, Mother of Jesus
Matthew: 1:16, 18-25; 2:11, 13-15, 19-21; 13:55-56
Mark: 3:21, 31-35; 6:3
Luke: 1:26-56; 2:1-52; 11:27-28; 23:49
John: 2:1-5, 12; 19:25-27
Acts: 1:14

John, The Beloved Disciple
Matthew: 4:21-22; 10:2-4; 17:1-9; 26:36-46; 27:55-56
Mark: 1:19-20, 29-31; 3:13-19; 5:35-43; 9:2-8, 38-41; 10:35-45;
    13:1-8; 14:32-42; 15:40; 16:1
Luke: 5:9-11; 6:13-16; 8:49-56; 9:28-36, 49-50, 52-56; 22:7-13
John: 13:21-30; 18:15-18; 19:25-27; 20:2-10, 19-23; 21:1-14, 20-
    25
Acts: 1:12-14; 3:1-11; 4:13-22; 8:14-17; 12:1-5
Galatians: 2:7-10
Revelation: 1.1-9, 21.1-5(?), 22.8-10
John 1, 2, and 3